D1539643

This Journal Belongs to:

_____

From the Author

For my husband, Art, a wise and godly man of prayer.

From the Illustrator

To Liana—I thank God for such an
incredible wife and friend.

Unless otherwise indicated, Bible verses are from the *International Children's Bible,
New Century Version* (ICB), copyright © 1983, 1986, 1988, 1999
by Tommy Nelson, a division of Thomas Nelson, Inc.

Quotations marked CEV are from *The Promise: The Contemporary English Version,*
copyright © 1995 by Thomas Nelson Inc.

ISBN 0-8499-5989-9 (Blue)

ISBN 0-8499-5982-9 (Green)

Printed in the United States of America.

00 01 02 03 RRD 9 8 7 6 5 4 3 2

My Prayer Journal

Written by

Karen Hill

Illustrations by

Bobby Gombert

Tommy
NELSON™

Thomas Nelson, Inc.
Nashville

Contents

Introduction

Dear Friend,

Welcome to *My Prayer Journal!* I'm glad you and I are going to spend some time together in the pages of this book. As we walk along together, we'll share some ideas about prayer. Throughout this journal, you'll read prayers that were prayed by people in the Bible. You'll find pages to help you think about why we pray and how we pray. And I've included journal space for you to write your own prayers.

My prayer for you is that this book will help you learn to love praying to your heavenly Father. By the time you're done, I hope prayer will be an important part of your everyday life.

How does this book work? First, this isn't a book you must go through from front to back. You can start working in it anywhere. The contents pages list prayer topics. So, if you want to pray about being lonely, turn to the chapter titled "A Prayer When I'm Lonely." If something good happens in your life, turn to "A Prayer of Thanks."

Also, there are pages with suggestions (how to talk to God about a certain topic), journal pages, and the pages with blue borders have prayer thoughts to encourage you and help you understand all about prayer.

At the end of the book is a very special section titled "My Prayer Path." Each time you pray about something, make a note of it in your Prayer Path. Then, each week, think about your prayers. When you feel that God has answered one of your prayers, flip over to the Prayer Path and write about it on the "answers" side. You may be surprised to see how God is working in your life.

Are you ready to pray? Before you begin, here's my prayer for you.

Dear Heavenly Father,

You are a great and wonderful God! I love you very much.

Thank you for letting me share some prayer ideas with my young friend.

Please, Father, help me to write clearly and help me know what to say on every page. I ask you to bless this book and the hands that will write special prayers to you. Thank you for listening to all the prayers of the person holding this book. Most of all, thank you for the gift of your Son, Jesus.

In Jesus' name,

Amen.

Now, turn the page to begin your journey of prayer!

Your friend,

Karen Hill

P.S. I'd love to hear about your *Prayer Journey.* You can write to me at:

Tommy Nelson™
P.O. Box 141000
Nashville, Tennessee 37214

What Is Prayer, Anyway?

Before you get started, let's talk a bit about prayer.

- Why do we pray?
- How do we pray?
- And, what is prayer, anyway?

Well, here's what prayer *isn't:*

Prayer is *not:*
- just memorizing words from a prayer book;
- something mysterious that only grownups can do;
- saying a few words before you gobble down your dinner;
- a lucky charm or a magic chant.

So, what *is* prayer?

Prayer *is:*
- having a conversation with your heavenly Father;
- telling God that you love him;
- sharing with God all the things that are in your heart;
- thanking God for the wonderful blessings he has given you;
- growing close to God by sharing this private, quiet time together.

Prayer *is* talking to God. Just like talking to your mom or dad or the person who takes care of you. And, when you pray, you don't have to use fancy words or pray at one certain time each day! God *really* wants to hear what's on your mind.

What do you talk to God about? Some of the things you can pray about include:

- what you are happy about;
- what you are worried about;
- what makes you afraid;
- what your dreams are for your life.

The best thing is that talking to God every day means you're walking through life with your heavenly Father by your side. The more you pray, the more you'll understand how important it is to be close to God. And praying every day means you are going through every moment of life—the good times, bad times, and in-between times—with God right there with you.

So, don't wait another minute. Your heavenly Father wants to hear from you!

Prayer Pieces

There aren't any rules for praying, but there are certain things that your prayers should include:

1. Some words that show God how much you love and respect him. Let him know that you believe he really is the one and only God and that you will try to obey him.

2. Confess to your heavenly Father the mistakes you've made that have hurt others or disappointed him or harmed yourself.

3. Spend some time sharing with God your needs or the needs of others. This is called "supplication."

4. Remind God that you belong to him and that you want to follow his will. Ask him to reveal his will to you clearly.

Here's an easy way to remember the "pieces of prayer":

P— Praise God. Thank him for his goodness and all the blessings he gives you.

R— Report your sins. Request God's forgiveness if you have hurt someone or disappointed him.

A— Ask for your needs and the needs of others.

Y— Yield. Give your prayers to your heavenly Father and trust him to listen to you and answer your prayers.

Remember the pieces of prayer:
P—Praise
R—Report
A—Ask
Y—Yield

THE BIBLE SHOWS US
How to Pray Like Jesus

Jesus' followers asked him to teach them how to pray. This is the prayer he prayed:

"Our Father in heaven,
We pray that your name will always be kept holy.
We pray that your kingdom will come.
We pray that what you want will be done,
  here on earth as it is in heaven.
Give us the food we need for each day.
Forgive the sins we have done,
  just as we have forgiven those who did wrong to us.
Do not cause us to be tested; but save us from the Evil One."

MATTHEW 6:9–13

Following Jesus' Example

Below is how the Lord's Prayer might look today:

Heavenly Father,
You are awesome!
I pray that everyone will say you are the true God.
I'm excited to think that one day I will get to live in heaven with you, and all the bad things of this world will go away forever.
Father, you're in charge of my life! I pray that you will help me do the things you want me to do (and everybody else, too!).
Please, God, make sure we have all the things we need, like plenty to eat, a place to live, and family and friends.
And one more thing, Father. Please forgive me. I've done some bad stuff. It's no secret from you, because you know everything that I do. But I hope you can forgive me. I'm sorry.
Help me remember that you've forgiven me. When someone hurts me, help me forgive them quickly.
Please keep Satan away from me. He's up to no good, and I really don't want him around!
Amen.

Praying Like Jesus

Now, you give it a try. Follow Jesus' example, but put his prayer in your own words:

Dear God,

_____

_____

_____

_____

_____

_____

_____

Amen.

Making God Smile

What happens to your mom's face when you hand her a fresh-picked flower? Her whole face seems to smile, doesn't it?

What happens to your dad's face when you do a chore without being asked? His face seems to turn into a big grin!

And what happens to your teacher's face when you turn in your homework on time? Her face suddenly looks years younger!

Why is that? Because you know that the way to change a frown to a smile is a gift from your heart. That's what a prayer of praise is—a gift to God.

It's the same with your heavenly Father. He hopes you'll choose to talk with him in prayer today, but sometimes you get too busy or tired or forgetful. So when you remember to talk to God, he is very happy to hear from you. In your own words and in your own way, just share with him what's on your mind.

And when you start your prayer by praising all the good things about him, you're putting a smile on his face as big as Jupiter!

Imagine your heavenly Father smiling each time you say, "Dear Father in heaven, I'd like to talk for a while. . . ."

THE BIBLE SHOWS US
How to Pray with Praise

In Jesus' example of a prayer, he praised his Father. Our prayers should always include some words of praise to God. Just tell him how great he is and how he has blessed your life. Here are some examples from the Bible:

"We will celebrate and praise you, Lord! You are good to us, and your love never fails. No one can praise you enough for all of the mighty things you have done."

PSALM 106:1–2, CEV

"I love you, Lord. You are my strength. The Lord is my rock, my protection, my Savior. My God is my rock. I can run to him for safety. He is my shield and my saving strength, my high tower. I will call to the Lord. He is worthy of praise."

PSALM 18:1–3

A Prayer of Praise

"I will praise you, Lord, with all my heart and tell about the wonders you have worked. God Most High, I will rejoice; I will celebrate and sing because of you."

PSALM 9:1–2, CEV

King David wrote many special prayers (called *psalms*). If a busy king can find time for praising God, I can, too!

Great and Wonderful Heavenly Father,

I'm bringing you a gift of praise today! I hope you like it.

I praise your name because you are a good God. You made our world, and you made us. You take care of us and give us everything we need.

I praise you most of all for sending your Son, Jesus. Because he came and because he died and because he rose again, I know that all my sins are forgiven.

Hooray!
Amen.

16

Dear Lord,
   Listen to the praises I have for you:

   You are:

   _____

   _____

   You did:

   _____

   _____

   I'm glad about:

   _____

   _____

Thank you!
Amen.

A Prayer of Thanks

"Every good action and every perfect gift is from God."

JAMES 1:17

A prayer is like a friendly letter for God. What should I put in my heavenly letter? All the reasons I think God is so great, that's what!

When I send God a prayer of thankfulness, it's like a special delivery praise straight from my heart. Here is my prayer of thankfulness:

Dear Heavenly Father,

You are a great God, and I love you! You made the mountains, the oceans, the prairies, and the rivers.

Only a powerful God could do such things. And you made me! I'm sure glad you decided to do that! You do many wonderful things for me—you bless me every day.

Thanks for loving me so much.

Amen.

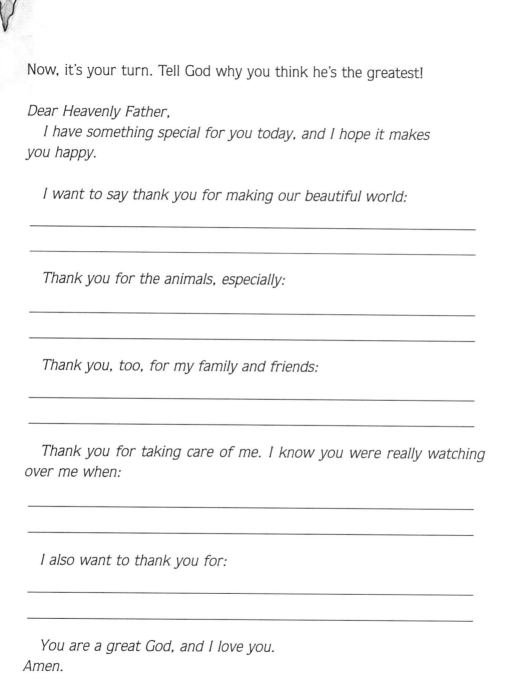

Now, it's your turn. Tell God why you think he's the greatest!

Dear Heavenly Father,
I have something special for you today, and I hope it makes you happy.

I want to say thank you for making our beautiful world:

_____

_____

Thank you for the animals, especially:

_____

_____

Thank you, too, for my family and friends:

_____

_____

Thank you for taking care of me. I know you were really watching over me when:

_____

_____

I also want to thank you for:

_____

_____

You are a great God, and I love you.
Amen.

A Prayer When I'm Happy

"I thank you from my heart, and I will never stop singing your praises, my Lord and my God."

PSALM 30:12, CEV

What a super day! I feel like shouting or singing or . . . maybe, praying! I want to share my joy with my heavenly Father. After all, he created the joy, so he and I should celebrate together!

Dear God,

I'm so happy today! I have so many reasons for being happy. Family, friends, great things happening all around—thank you, Father, for all you do in my life. And even when things aren't going so well, I'm happy deep down, because I know you love me and care about me. And most of all, you're in my heart, so you're sharing my happy day.
Amen.

Dear God,

Thank you for helping me have such a great day. I'm happy about:

_____

_____

And also, I'm happy about:

_____

_____

Here's something that made me feel special today:

_____

_____

Father, I hope you're happy today, too!

I love you.
Amen.

A Prayer for Our Beautiful World

"Praise the Lord from the earth. Praise him, you large sea animals and all the oceans. Praise him, lightning and hail, snow and clouds, and stormy winds that obey him. Praise him, mountains and all hills, fruit trees and all cedar trees. Praise him, you wild animals and all cattle, small crawling animals and birds."

PSALM 148:7–10

Monkeys in trees,
Buzzy buzzy bees,
Birds that tweet,
Bugs that creep . . .

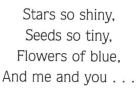 Creatures that run and critters that crawl—
Our heavenly Father made them all!

Stars so shiny,
Seeds so tiny,
Flowers of blue,
And me and you . . .

Winter, summer, spring, fall,
God in heaven made them all!

Dear God,

It must be fun to look down from heaven and see all the things you've made. Mountains, rivers, bears, and ants—what a creator you are! You are awesome, and so are all your creations!

Please help us know how to take care of the beautiful world you made for us.

Amen.

Dear God,

Thank you for making:

_____

Some of my favorite things I enjoy in your beautiful world are:

_____

Thanks for creating me, too! Here are some reasons I'm glad you made me:

_____

_____

Amen.

A Prayer for My Pets

"Then God said, 'Let the earth be filled with animals.'"
GENESIS 1:24

Goldfish in tanks, hamsters in cages, puppies rolling on the floor, shy cats, even turtles and snakes—God made pets of every size and color. Pets that bark and pets that sing—our heavenly Father thought of everything!

Dear Heavenly Father,

I'm so glad you thought of pets! Animals make such good friends—they always love, no matter what. If I have a bad day at school, my pet is still glad to see me when I come home. Thank you for pets, heavenly Father. I'll do my best to take care of the pets in my life.
Amen.

If you don't have a pet, talk to God about the kind of pet you'd like to have someday. If you do have a pet, thank God and tell him all the reasons you are grateful for this blessing.

Dear Heavenly Father,

_____

_____

_____

_____

Amen.

STOP

Mention your prayer for your pet in your Prayer Path.

A Prayer for My Friends

"I pray that God will be kind to you. . . ."
1 PETER 1:2, CEV

I can barely comprehend
Why God gave me such a friend.
We laugh and talk and share our dreams.
In good times or bad, we're a team.
What a blessing, let me state,
Friendship is oh, so great!

Dear Heavenly Father,

A friend is a great blessing! I know you placed this special person in my life, and I'm very thankful to you. Please watch over my friend. When my friend has problems, show me how to help. Or if I just need to be a good listener, help me do that, too.

Thanks again for giving me the gift of a good friend.
Amen.

My prayer about a special friend:

Dear God,
*   I want to talk to you about my special friend, _____.*
Thank you for bringing _____ into my life.
*   Thank you for giving us fun times together, like the time we*

_____

_____

*   Please bless my friend in this way:*

_____

_____

*   Please help me be a good friend.*
Amen.

STOP

Check your Prayer
Path. Make a
note of any
answered prayers.

A Prayer for My Whole Family

"We always remember you when we pray and thank God for all of you."

1 THESSALONIANS 1:2

A family is not just moms and dads, brothers and sisters. A family is aunts, uncles, grandparents, and cousins. Whether a family is large or small, near or far away, a family is a gift of God. I want to pray every day for these people who love me more than anyone else in the world.

Dear Heavenly Father,

You didn't stop when you created the world. You didn't stop when you made the animals, birds, and fish. You didn't stop when you created Adam. You knew he would be lonely, so you gave him a family. And since then, you've made so many families—all different kinds of families. Some are small, and some are large. But families are your idea, so I know you care about them.

I'm glad to have people who love me. Thank you for my family,
Father. I pray you'll take care of my family.
Amen.

Write a special prayer about your family.

Dear Father,

   Thank you for my family. Please bless _____ and

_____ and _____

   Here are some special requests for my family:

_____

_____

_____

_____

_____

Amen.

STOP

Flip over to the
Prayer Path in the
back of the book.
Make a note of
your prayers for
your family.

Our Forgiving Father

My family and I were on a camping trip. As Daddy unloaded the car, he said, "Stay near the cabin; don't wander off." As you can guess, it didn't take me long to do just that. I couldn't wait to walk through the woods and look for squirrels and wildflowers. So, I wandered off. Big time. Before long, I couldn't see the cabin. I couldn't remember the way back. My father's words echoed in my heart. Not only had I disobeyed him, but I wondered if I'd ever see him again. I was lost.

I ran through the woods, trying to find a familiar path. But nothing looked the same. Then I saw a house in a clearing. *Maybe someone there will help me,* I thought. But as I neared the house, a big, mean dog started chasing me. I ran to a fence and started climbing. Then, crying and thinking I was lost forever, I saw a wonderful sight. Running down the hill toward me was my daddy. He pulled me over the top of the fence.

Do you think my father reminded me that I'd disobeyed? Did he say he wouldn't love me anymore? No. He held me tight and told me I was safe. He told me he loved me and that he would always watch out for me.

You know, that story reminds me of another father—our heavenly Father. When we disobey him, he doesn't become angry at us. He, like my daddy, doesn't take his love away. He does what any loving father would do: He forgives us.

When you've made mistakes, when you've done things you know are wrong, talk to your heavenly Father. He is watching out for you and ready to comfort you.

How to Pray for Forgiveness

Daniel and his friends had been captured by a king who had taken over their country. The king and his people disobeyed God and lived lives that did not please their heavenly Father. Daniel was a good man, prayerful and obedient to God's ways. But because he loved God and his country, he prayed for forgiveness for all the people.

"Listen to my prayer for help. . . . We do not ask these things because we are good. We ask because of your mercy. Lord, listen! Lord, forgive!"
DANIEL 9:17–19

A Prayer for Forgiveness

"I prayed to the Lord my God. I told him about all of my sins."

Daniel 9:4

I knew it was wrong, but I did it anyway. I did something I'm not proud of doing. In fact, I'm sure that it didn't please God. I should pray about this right away!

Dear Heavenly Father,

You are my God and I love you. I want to do the things that make you happy. But sometimes I mess up. I'm very sorry, Father. Will you please forgive me?

I have something I want to confess to you:

____

____

____

____

____

Thank you for listening to me.
Amen.

Dear God,

Here are some other things I want to tell you. I'm so sorry that I:

_____

_____

_____

_____

_____

I know that I do things that aren't right sometimes. Father, please help me stop doing these things:

_____

_____

_____

_____

_____

_____

_____

Amen.

A Prayer When I'm Angry

"Do not go on being angry all day."
EPHESIANS 4:26

"Losing your temper is foolish."
PROVERBS 12:16, CEV

I'm really mad. In fact, I'm so mad I can hardly think.
If you knew what happened, you'd be angry, too!
But being angry makes me feel awful!
I want to quit being angry—
I better pray about it before I bust!

Dear God,
*   I know you don't like anger. It*
sure doesn't do any good. But I'm
having a hard time handling my
angry feelings. God, I'm
sorry, really sorry that
my anger made me act
foolishly. Please forgive
me. Please help me
work this out.
Amen.

In your own words, explain what's going on that made you angry. Share everything with God, and then wait for him to help you let it go.

Dear Father,

_____

_____

_____

_____

_____

_____

Amen.

Turn to your
Prayer Path.
Write your request
about not
getting angry.

A Prayer to Help Me Tell the Truth

"So you must stop telling lies. Tell each other the truth. . . ."
EPHESIANS 4:25

Okay, I know it's wrong to lie. But sometimes it's scary to tell the truth. Maybe I'll get in trouble. Maybe my parents will be disappointed. Maybe no one will trust me again. I really want to be truthful. It's going to take some heavenly help to get me on the right track.

Dear Heavenly Father,

It's me again. I'm a bit ashamed to admit this, but sometimes I have trouble being truthful. I know telling lies doesn't please you, so I'm praying for your help about this problem. Help me be strong when I need to tell the truth.

Amen.

Have you told a lie? Confess it to your heavenly Father (and to anyone else who needs to hear the truth). This may not be easy, but it will make it easier to be truthful next time.

Dear Father,
I'm sorry that I wasn't truthful about:

_____

_____

_____

_____

_____

_____

_____

Amen.

STOP

Put a note in your Prayer Path about asking God to help you stay truthful.

A Prayer When I Make Mistakes

"We are very weak, but the Spirit helps us with our weakness. We do not know how to pray as we should. But the Spirit himself speaks to God for us, even begs God for us. . . . God can see what is in people's hearts."

ROMANS 8:26–27

Why did I do it? How could I have made such a big mistake? Does God still love me when I mess up?

Dear God,

I'm sad and glad at the same time. Does that make sense? My heart hurts to know I disappointed you. But I'm happy to know that you love me, no matter how many times I make mistakes. This is a great blessing. And because you'll never give up on me, I won't give up on me, either. I'll try to do better next time!

Amen.

Talk to God about your mistakes. Then let him forgive you and you forgive yourself.

Dear God,

You are my God, and I want to please you. I've done some things that are wrong. Here is what's on my heart today:

_____

_____

Please forgive me for:

_____

_____

_____

Amen.

Just a Prayer Away

A little boy was trying to help his mom carry in the groceries. He picked up the biggest sack. The bag dropped out of his arms. Crash! Broken ketchup bottle. Scrambled eggs! Apples and oranges rolling across the kitchen floor like ants scurrying at a picnic. What a mess!

The little boy wanted to cry. Then his mom spoke. "I'm glad you wanted to help. But the sack was too heavy for you. All you had to do was ask, and I would've helped you."

"All you had to do was *ask*."

That is what God wants us to do: ask. That's why he invented prayer. He has promised that he will always listen when his children pray to him. We may not always understand God's answers to our prayers. Sometimes he says yes; sometimes he says no; and sometimes he wants us to be patient and wait. But we can be certain that he hears us and that he cares.

In other words, be brave in your prayers. Tell your Father your heart's desires. Now, that doesn't mean we should pray "Give me a million dollars" or "Make so-and-so move to another town because he's mean to me." But remember this: No request is too small for God. He's interested in everything about your life—at home, at school, at the ballpark, everywhere you are.

So, be brave in prayer. Like the little boy, some of your concerns are too heavy for you to carry alone. Let God carry them for you.

All you have to do is *ask!*

THE BIBLE SHOWS US
How to Pray for Help

One purpose of prayer is to ask for God's help. He will always listen. Below are some examples of Bible prayers for help.

"But I pray to you, Lord. So when the time is right, answer me and help me with your wonderful love."

PSALM 69:13, CEV

"Please listen, Lord! Answer my prayer for help. When I am in trouble, I pray, knowing you will listen."

PSALM 86:6–7, CEV

"Lord my God, I trust in you for protection. Save me and rescue me. . . ."

PSALM 7:1

A Prayer to Help Me Grow Close to God

"The Lord is close to everyone who prays to him, to all who truly pray to him."

PSALM 145:18

I know God has a plan for me. I want to live a life that pleases him. But how will I know what to do? I'll trust God to help me understand him better as he and I talk often in prayer.

Dear Heavenly Father,

Being close to you is important to me. I want to know you better and to understand your will in my life.

Father, I'm going to be quiet for a few minutes. Instead of talking, I'll just listen awhile. Perhaps you'll speak to my heart.

Amen.

Dear Father,
Here are some ways you can help me feel close to you:

_____

When I'm afraid, help me:

_____

When I'm confused, help me:

_____

Here are some other ways:

_____

Amen.

A Prayer to Help Me Be a Good Sport

"Those who want to do right more than anything else are happy."

MATTHEW 5:6

Winning feels great, but sometimes I forget to say something nice to the loser.

Losing doesn't feel so hot, and sometimes it makes me think bad thoughts and act like a bad sport.

I want to be a kind winner and a good loser. Those are two big jobs!

Dear Father,
I want to please you by the way I win and lose. If I'm kind to the loser, others will see Jesus in me. If I lose with a good attitude, Jesus will shine through, too. Will you help me remember to think about being a good sport before *the game? Help me have a winning attitude toward my opponents!*
Amen.

Dear Father,

I want to talk about winning and losing—what it feels like, and how I should behave.

_____

_____

_____

_____

_____

_____

Amen.

STOP

Prayer Path: Ask God to help you be kind to others when they lose.

A Prayer to Help Me Worship

"Lord our Master, your name is the most wonderful name in all the earth! It brings you praise in heaven above. You have taught children and babies to sing praises to you."

PSALM 8:1–2

Is worship a once-a-week activity? Is it something I can only do in church with a crowd of people? No way! I don't have to wait for church—I can worship God each day!

Worship on Sunday,
Talk to God on Monday,
Praise his name on Tuesday,
Tell others about him on Wednesday,
Ask for his help on Thursday,
Thank him for his blessings on Friday,
Sing a song of praise on Saturday,
Start over again on Sunday!

Dear God,
  I worship you. You are my God.
  I will worship you all my life.
  I worship you because:

_____

_____

_____

_____

_____

_____

_____

Amen.

A Prayer to Help Me
Care about Others

"Love each other. You must love each other as I have loved you."
JOHN 13:34

"So never think that some people are more important than others."
JAMES 2:1

Jesus said caring about others shows that we care about him. I'm not really sure what he wants me to do, but I'll pray that God will help me know how to care.

Dear Father,

All people were created by you. That means you love everyone else as much as you love me. Even the mean kid at school. Even people who act like they don't love you. Help me learn to love all kinds of people, even people I don't like very much. Help me show your love for them by being kind.

Amen.

Create a prayer about caring for others. If you know some people who are handicapped or have special needs, be sure to ask for God's blessings on them.

Dear Heavenly Father,

_____

_____

_____

_____

_____

Amen.

STOP

Put a note in your Prayer Path about people with special needs. Ask God to bless them today and to show you how to be kind to them.

A Prayer to Help Me Understand Death

"Don't be worried! Have faith in God and have faith in me. There are many rooms in my Father's house. . . . I am going there to prepare a place for each of you."

JOHN 14:1–2, CEV

I have so many questions. Why do people die? Why does it hurt so much when someone I love dies? Why does God sometimes seem silent when I'm searching for answers? I know God wants me to trust him about this. But I need his help to trust.

Dear God,

Your ways are hard to understand sometimes. I know heaven is a wonderful home. And I know you have a special place there for all people who believe in you. But I don't like it when someone I love has to die. It's hard to say good-bye, even though I know the person is in heaven with you.

Will my heart ever stop hurting? Will I ever understand how to be peaceful when someone dies? Will I always miss them this much?

I need your comfort, Lord. I really do.

Amen.

Talk to God about death. Let him know your questions, your fears. Then let him comfort you.

Dear Father,
Even though I'm sad, I want to say that I love and trust you. You are a great God because:

_____

_____

I thank you that _____ was a part of my life. These are some things that I loved about him/her:

_____

_____

Here are my questions about death:

_____

_____

Father, please bless me and stay close to me right now.
Amen.

A Prayer to Help Me
Be a Good Friend

"You should try as much as you can to add these things to your lives:
. . . kindness for your brothers and sisters in Christ."

2 PETER 1:5–7

What's the best way to be a good friend?
Pray for each other day out, day in.
In good times or bad, happy or sad,
I'll send a prayer to my heavenly Dad!

Dear Father,

I'm grateful for my special friend. Thank you for sending someone so great my way! I pray you will keep my friend safe and healthy. And please give us lots of good times together. If we ever disagree, help me be the first one to say, "I'm sorry." And last, but not least, will you show me how to be a good friend?

Your friend,
Me

Tell God all about your friend:

Dear Father,

_____

_____

_____

_____

_____

_____

_____

_____

_____

Amen.

A Pocketful of Prayers

One warm spring day, my one-year-old granddaughter and I went for a walk. Shelby toddled along, exploring the grass, wildflowers, dirt, and leaves. She was excited to discover some pebbles, so I slipped one into the pocket of her dress. Wonder of wonders! She didn't even know she had a pocket, and she certainly didn't realize that it could hold her little treasures. It was a happy discovery for her.

But then she began to worry that she would lose her rock. Every few steps, she would stop and peek in her pocket. Then she'd see that her rock was still there, and she'd giggle, and off she'd go again.

Shelby and her pocket-rock remind me of big people. Sometimes, since we can't actually see God's face, we wonder if he's still there. Doubts begin to creep in, and we wonder if he's listening to us. Especially when we go through tough or sad times. When that happens, remember the promise of 1 John 4:12–13 (CEV): "If we love each other, God lives in us, and his love is truly in our hearts. God has given us his Spirit. That is how we know that we are one with him, just as he is one with us." Reach into your pocketful of prayers and remember, no matter what, God is with you.

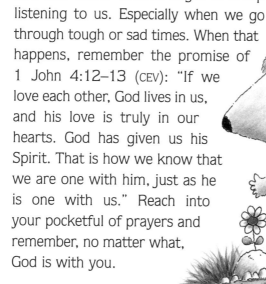

THE BIBLE SHOWS US
How to Pray for Faith

When we have doubts about God and his ways, we should ask him to help us be strong in our faith . . . to trust him more. Here are some Bible examples of praying for faith:

"I will listen to you, Lord God, because you promise peace to those who are faithful and no longer foolish. You are ready to rescue everyone who worships you, so that you will live with us in all of your glory."
PSALM 85:8–9, CEV

"Teach me to follow you, and I will obey your truth. Always keep me faithful. With all my heart I thank you. I praise you, Lord God."
PSALM 86:11–12, CEV

"Please listen, Lord, and answer my prayer! . . . I trust you. Be kind to me! I pray to you all day. Make my heart glad! I serve you, and my prayer is sincere."
PSALM 86:1–4, CEV

A Prayer to Help Me Act Like Jesus

"In your lives you must think and act like Christ Jesus."

Philippians 2:5

That's a big dream: wanting to act like Jesus. But with God's help, I can try. Where should I start? Growing a heart that loves other people seems like the right place to begin. If I can learn to love others, maybe God's light will shine through me.

Dear Father,

Your Son was perfect. I know I can't be perfect like him, but I'd like to try. Will you show me how to love other people? Will you help me be more kind and patient with the people in my life? Will you help me try to do what Jesus would do?

Amen.

Write a prayer that tells how you want to be like Jesus.

Dear God,

    Jesus was perfect. He never did:

_____

_____

    He always:

_____

_____

    I'm not perfect. Please help me to:

_____

_____

Amen.

57

A Prayer for God to Be with Me

"Remain in me and follow my teachings. If you do this, then you can ask for anything you want, and it will be given to you."

JOHN 15:7

My life is like a path. Up a hill, down into the valley, through the dark woods, and out into the sunshine. On my journey, there are many roads to choose. Sometimes, I'm not sure which path to take, but God is there to guide me. If I listen, I will take the right path.

Dear Father,

Thank you for loving me enough to walk along with me through life.

Please guide me and show me the way to go.

Amen.

Talk to God about the path of your life, about growing up and the decisions you'll make. Tell him about your dreams and ask him to guide you every step of the way.

Dear God,

You are my God and I praise you for loving me. Thank you for:

_____

Please forgive me for:

_____

I know you care about what happens in my life. Help me know your will about:

_____

Amen.

A Prayer for Morning

"Lord, every morning you hear my voice. Every morning, I tell you what I need. And I wait for your answer."

PSALM 5:3

What a great way to start the day! Before I head for school, I'll have a chat with my heavenly Father. I'll call it my morning exercise—keeping my heart in good shape.

Good Morning, Heavenly Father!

Thanks for a good night's rest. And thank you for starting the day with me. There's a lot on my mind this morning. Today, I'm going to tell you about my schedule for the day.

Please be with me every minute. Let me know that you're there.

We'll talk again later.

Amen.

Tell your Father about the day ahead:

Dear Father,

_____

_____

_____

_____

_____

_____

_____

Amen.

A Prayer for Bedtime

"I praise the Lord because he guides me. Even at night, I feel his leading. I keep the Lord before me always. Because he is close by my side I will not be hurt."

PSALM 16:7–8

Better than a night-light . . . I have a heavenly Father to watch over me while I sleep. He's always on duty, even while I'm dreaming.

Dear Father,

Thank you for protecting me while I sleep. It's good to know I don't have to worry about monsters and other creepy, spooky things. You're watching and keeping me safe.

I love sleeping in your strong arms.

Thank you for taking care of my sleeping hours.

Amen.

My bedtime prayer:

Dear Heavenly Father,
Let me thank you for:

_____

_____

Today I did these things:

_____

_____

_____

Now I'll say good night. Thank you for protecting me while I sleep. Amen.

Abba Time

When Jesus prayed, he called his heavenly Father "Abba." In our language that means "Daddy."

Can you imagine calling God "Daddy"? He wants you to.

Even more, can you imagine climbing up in your heavenly Father's lap to talk? He wants you to.

Though you can't see his face, you are in your Abba's presence every time you pray. And he's so glad you're there!

The Bible tells us that Jesus prayed often. And many times, he prayed alone. He would go off by himself to a quiet place and talk to his Abba for hours.

You can do the same. Oh, you don't have to go up on a mountain. Just find some quiet place where you and Abba can visit alone.

Try to find a way to have this quiet time every single day. Early in the morning or after school or before bedtime. Give up a favorite TV show and let that be your "Abba Time." Or go out to play *after* your Abba Time. Let God know he's important to you by setting aside time just for him.

Your Abba—your "heavenly Daddy"—wants you to!

THE BIBLE SHOWS US
How to Pray for Courage

"Have courage. May the Lord be with those who do what is right."

2 CHRONICLES 19:11

After Moses died, a man named Joshua became the leader of his people. It was a big job—he had to show thousands of people how to move to their new land. Joshua didn't think he could do it. But as he prayed to God about it, he felt that God really wanted him to do this job. God said to Joshua, ". . . be strong and brave. . . . don't be afraid. The Lord your God will be with you everywhere you go" (Joshua 1:9).

God encouraged Joshua. Look at the word that is tucked inside "encourage"—it's *courage!* So, when you feel small and weak like Joshua, pray that God will give you courage, just as he did for this soldier so long ago.

A Prayer When I'm Lonely

"Turn to me and be kind to me. I am lonely and hurting."
PSALM 25:16

Sometimes I feel invisible, because it seems that no one notices me. Doesn't anyone want to be my friend? It's really tough to keep a strong attitude when I feel so lonely. Maybe it will help to spend some time in prayer.

Dear Father,

Your Bible tells me that you're always listening. Knowing that you care makes me feel better. I'm sure glad you're here to talk to. Father, can you help me? This is a lonely time for me because _____

_____

_____ .

Thank you for reminding me that I'm special to you because you made me. What a wonderful Father you are!
Amen.

Dear God,

Thank you for listening to my prayer. I'm especially glad you're listening, because today I'm feeling lonely. Here's what it feels like:

_____

_____

This is what happened to make me feel this way:

_____

_____

I would like to change this feeling, because:

_____

_____

Father, please help me remember that you are with me, even on days like this.
Amen.

STOP

Time to check your Prayer Path.
Look at answered prayers and
make a note of your prayer
about being lonely.

A Prayer When I'm Afraid

"So, don't worry, because I am with you. Don't be afraid, because I am your God. I will make you strong and will help you . . ."

ISAIAH 41:10

Sometimes I'm afraid. And what's worse, then I start feeling kind of silly for being afraid. Being scared is bad enough, but I'm embarrassed to tell anyone. Is my heavenly Father listening? Will he help me quit being scared?

Dear Father,

I'll get right to the point. I'm scared. I can't seem to help it. Father, will you help me stop being so afraid? I trust you and I know you can help me. It's good to know that you never get tired of listening to me talk about my fears. I'll just sit quietly for a bit and think about how you'll help me be brave.

Amen.

Dear God,

It's good to be able to talk to you about this. You see, I'm scared about _____. This is how it makes me feel:

_____

_____

Remember, heavenly Father, how I used to be scared about:

_____

_____

Thank you for helping me get over being scared. This is how you helped me:

_____

_____

Thanks for listening, Father.
In Jesus' name,
Amen.

STOP

Flip over to the Prayer Path at the back of the book. Make a note of your prayer about being afraid.

A Prayer When I'm Confused

"Please make me wise and teach me the difference between right and wrong."
1 KINGS 3:9, CEV

Should I play in the band or do sports? Should I change my haircut? Should I do my homework or watch TV? Should I go here, or should I go there? Should I spend time with this friend or that friend? My head is spinning with all these choices. I feel mixed up and confused. Help!

Dear Heavenly Father,
I sure need you today. You are great and strong and smart, and I'm just a kid who's very confused. Sometimes it seems I should make a certain choice. Then I'm not sure.
Help me know what to do, Father. Thanks!
Amen.

Dear Heavenly Father,

I'm so mixed up. Some people tell me one thing, and others tell me just the opposite. I want to do the right thing. I sure need your help. Here is what I'm trying to figure out:

_____

_____

_____

_____

_____

Please, Father, help me make good choices. Help me know what you would like for me to do. I know you will lead me toward the right decisions. Amen.

In the Prayer Path at the back of the book, write about a choice you have to make.

A Prayer to Help Me Get Along with Others

"Don't let your hearts be troubled."
JOHN 14:27

Arguing makes me feel awful. It makes my stomach hurt. My palms get sweaty. I really want to do better at getting along with others.

Dear Father,
I don't like arguing, and I don't think you like it, either. I need your help. I'm not sure how to get along better with others, but I believe you can help me. I trust you, Lord, to work on my heart and help me be kinder to others.
Amen.

Pour out your heart to God about this problem. You've got the whole next page to tell him all about it.

Dear Heavenly Father,

Thank you for listening to me. I need to talk to you about how tough it is to always get along with others. Here is how it feels:

_____

_____

_____

_____

_____

Please help me with:

_____

_____

_____

_____

_____

Amen.

STOP

Prayer Path
note: Ask God
to bring peace
to your
relationships.

A Prayer When I'm Sad

"We know that in everything God works for the good of those who love him."

ROMANS 8:28

My heart's about to break. I wonder if anyone else has ever felt like this? I wonder how I can go on, feeling this sad. When the sadness makes my world seem as dark as night, I'll try to remember that someone does know how my broken heart feels. Jesus had his heart broken many times: when people were cruel to him, when people didn't believe in him, when his friends pretended not to know him. But through it all, he talked often about how much he loved everyone. Maybe the love of Jesus will shine through my broken heart.

Dear Father in Heaven,

You are the creator of joy, so I know your heart hurts when your children are sad. I can almost feel your tears falling for me. I know you must have been sad when your Son, Jesus, had to die on the cross.

Thank you for helping me get through my sadness. Please, Father, help me remember that I'm never alone, because you are with me. Amen.

Tell God all the details. He wants to know everything that's on your heart, so he can help you get over your sad time.

Dear God,

_____

_____

_____

_____

_____

Amen.

A Prayer When Someone Is Mean to Me

"Do for other people the same things you want them to do for you."
MATTHEW 7:12

It wasn't right—it's never right for people to treat each other badly. I'm upset about what happened. I know God expects me to love my enemies. This is going to be hard! I'm going to need some prayer support right away to make things right!

Dear God,

I don't like being treated badly by people. It feels awful and makes me think bad thoughts about them.
I don't like feeling this way. Can you help?

Help me smile and act kindly toward the ones who were unkind to me. Help me remember that they are your children, too, and that we all make mistakes. Help me remember how often you've forgiven me for my mistakes.

Just show me how to forgive and love them. Amen.

Write down the whole story of what happened. Ask God to help you forgive and forget. Ask for his help to stop thinking about it so much.

Dear God,

_____

_____

_____

_____

_____

_____

_____

STOP

_____

Prayer Path: Mark down a special blessing for the one who treated you wrongly.

Amen.

Prayer Thoughts

The Coin Man

My friend Stanley is a missionary. He travels all over the world telling people about Jesus. He especially cares about the children of the world. Wherever he goes, he reminds young people to pray for children in other countries. He'll say, "I want you to pray for the children in Romania (or New Zealand or New York)." To help kids remember to pray, he gives them coins from other countries. If he meets a young person in Canada, he'll give that child a coin from Haiti, and say, "This coin will help you remember to pray for the children of Haiti every day." If he's in the Philippines, he'll hand out African coins, asking for prayers for the African children.

Some children have to face difficulties every day—wars and disease have hurt many families. They need your prayers. Stanley's not here to hand you a coin, so how can you choose a country to pray for? Here's an idea: Spin your globe or pull out a world map and let your finger land on a country. This will be your special country to pray about, asking God to help the children and bless them. Perhaps one day you'll meet someone from your "prayer country," and you can tell them about your prayers.

You can be sure that your heavenly Father cares as much for the children across the ocean as he does for you. And he is pleased to know that you care, too.

THE BIBLE SHOWS US
How to Pray for the World

"They will pray and obey me and stop their evil ways. If they do, I will hear them from heaven. I will forgive their sin, and I will heal their land."

2 CHRONICLES 7:14

When Moses led the people out of Egypt, they often behaved like crybabies! When things didn't go their way, they would complain and threaten to stop believing in God. Of course, this made God very sad and he wanted to punish the people. But Moses prayed on behalf of the people, and God listened and changed his mind.

"Moses begged the Lord his God. Moses said, 'Lord, don't let your anger destroy your people. You brought these people out of Egypt with your great power and strength'. . . . So the Lord changed his mind. He did not destroy the people" (Exodus 32:11, 14).

God loves all his people, even when they disobey. So when you pray for the world, ask God to keep his people away from sin, and ask for forgiveness when the world disobeys.

A Prayer for the World's Children

"'Let the little children come to me . . .' Then Jesus took the children in his arms. He put his hands on them and blessed them."

MARK 10:14–16

God has so many children! There are zillions of kids in China and Brazil and France and all the other countries. Since all the kids in the world belong to God, it means I have zillions of brothers and sisters all over the world. What a huge family I have!

Dear God,

It's awesome to think about all the kids around the world who belong to you. I know you love them as much as you love me.

Here's a special prayer for the children who might be hungry or scared because of wars in their country. Please keep them safe and see that they get enough food. And help them know that you love them, even when times are bad.

Thank you for listening. And thank you for caring for all your children. Amen.

Now, write your own prayer for the brothers and sisters in your "world family."

Dear Heavenly Father,
    Please bless the children around the world who know about you. Here are my special prayers about the kids in other countries:

_____

_____

_____

    For the children who don't know about you God, please help missionaries come to them and tell them your Good News!
    I especially want to pray for the children in this country:

_____

Amen.

STOP

Prayer Path time! Write your special requests
for children around the world.

A Prayer for Our Leaders

"You should pray for kings and for all who have authority. Pray for the leaders so that we can have quiet and peaceful lives—lives full of worship and respect for God."

1 Timothy 2:2

In our world, there are kings, queens, presidents, governors, princes, princesses, dictators, and leaders of all sorts. There are good ones, bad ones, weak ones, and strong ones. Some leaders believe in God and some don't. Some countries, like ours, are blessed with freedom. Others are troubled by wars. The Bible tells me to pray for the world's leaders, and I can see that they need my prayers.

Dear Father,

You are so good—you've given us a great country in which to live. Some countries are in trouble. There is fighting going on, and people are getting hurt. Father, I care about these problems, and I know you do, too.

Please, Father, listen to my prayer for the world's leaders. Turn their hearts to you. Make them try to stop fighting and arguing.

Help them love their neighbors and do good to others. Help them remember the Golden Rule.

In Jesus' name,

Amen.

Dear God,

I'm praying for all the leaders in the world today, especially in countries where there is fighting and people are hungry.

I want to pray for the leaders of our country. Here are some concerns I have about our country:

_____

_____

It must be hard to run a city. So please bless our city leaders, because:

_____

_____

Help our leaders to:

_____

Amen.

STOP

Turn to your Prayer Path at the back of the book.
Write down the leaders you prayed for today.

A Prayer for Those Who Don't Know Jesus

"For God loved the world so much that he gave his only Son. God gave his Son so that whoever believes in him may not be lost, but have eternal life."

JOHN 3:16

God loves all people, everywhere. And he wants each person to know about him. There are people in my neighborhood and my city who don't know Jesus. Oh, they've heard his name, but they don't know that he is the Son of God. And they don't know that he came to earth and died to save them. I can't tell everyone about Jesus, but here's something I can do: pray for them!

Dear Heavenly Father,

Today I'm praying for all the people in the world who haven't heard about you. I know these people are important to you. And I pray that somehow, someway, someday, they will come to know you.

Please bring people into their lives who can share the great news of Jesus with them.

I also want to pray for the missionaries who go to foreign countries to share the message. Please bless them on their journey of faith.

And, Father, I know some people who don't know about you. Help me be a good example to them. Help me know how to tell them about you. Amen.

Dear Father,

I want to pray today for people everywhere who don't know about you. I especially want to pray for these people in my neighborhood and in my life who don't know you:

_____

_____

And, for my friends who don't know about you:

_____

_____

Please bless them and make their hearts turn toward you. Amen.

STOP

This is an important prayer to record in your Prayer Path!

A Prayer for My Church

"God called you and chose you to be his. Try hard to show that you really are God's chosen people. . . ."

2 PETER 1:10

"You should try as much as you can to add these things to your lives: . . . to your service for God, add kindness for your brothers and sisters in Christ; and to this kindness, add love."

2 PETER 1:5, 7

A church is like a little peek into heaven: people who love God and love each other; teachers who share the Good News about Jesus and our someday-home in heaven; ministers who help people get through tough times; and members who show God's love to one another. A church should be full of love.

Dear God,

Thank you for my church. I'm grateful for the ministers, the teachers, the nursery workers, and the people who keep it clean. Thank you for helping us see what your love is like, by loving one another.

Help me know how to be a good example of your love to others in my church family.

Amen.

Dear Heavenly Father,
　　Thank you for my church. I'm especially thankful for:

_____

_____

　　Please protect my Christian brothers and sisters in my church. Some who really need your blessings right now are:

_____

_____

_____

　　Please help our church know how to tell others about you!
Amen.

STOP

Time to turn to your Prayer Path. Note your prayers for your church. (And while you're there, write down some answers you've received.)

Praying with a Friend

"I tell you that if two of you on earth agree about something, then you can pray for it."

MATTHEW **18:19**

A partner in prayer? What a cool idea! We can share what's in our hearts and talk to God together. It's good to know God will listen to my partner and me. Even when we're not together, we can agree to be praying about the same thing, and God will listen.

Dear Heavenly Father,

Will you help me find a prayer partner? Will you give me the courage to ask someone to pray with me today? And help me know the things that we should pray for today.

Amen.

Here are some things my prayer partner and I will pray about:

_____

_____

_____

_____

_____

_____

Write these requests in your Prayer Path
at the back of the book.

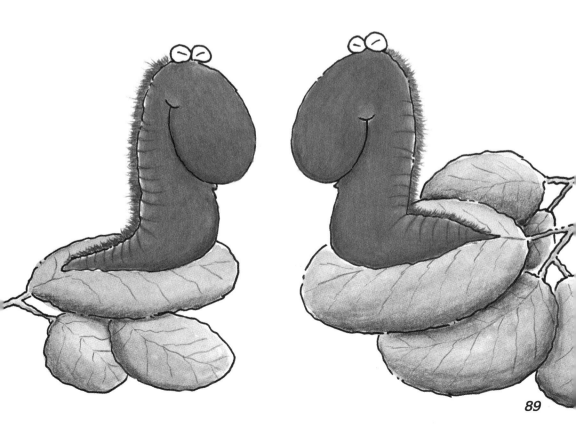

My Prayer of Promise

"Then you will call my name. You will come to me and pray to me. And I will listen to you. You will search for me. And when you search for me with all your heart, you will find me!"

JEREMIAH 29:12–13

There's one very special prayer you can pray to make Jesus a part of your life. You can tell him in your prayer that you believe in him and that you want to belong to him forever. He wants to be a part of your life. Here's what you might say:

Dear Father,

I love you and want to be your child. I believe that you are the only true God. I believe that Jesus is your Son and that he came to Earth and died on the cross to take away my sins.

I know that you love me, even though I've done things that haven't pleased you. Please forgive me for that.

Please come into my life. I want you to live in my heart every day, forever. Thank you for loving me.

Amen.

Talk to your heavenly Father about being his child. Ask him to guide you in your new walk together.

Dear God,

_____

_____

_____

_____

_____

_____

_____

Amen.

STOP

Prayer Path:
Write down this
important day, when
you promised your
heart to Jesus!!

My Prayer Path

DATE   I'M PRAYING ABOUT   HOW THIS PRAYER WAS ANSWERED

_____   _____   _____

             _____   _____

             _____   _____

DATE   I'M PRAYING ABOUT   HOW THIS PRAYER WAS ANSWERED

_____   _____   _____

             _____   _____

             _____   _____

DATE	I'M PRAYING ABOUT	HOW THIS PRAYER WAS ANSWERED
_____	_____ _____ _____	_____ _____ _____
DATE	I'M PRAYING ABOUT	HOW THIS PRAYER WAS ANSWERED
_____	_____ _____ _____	_____ _____ _____
DATE	I'M PRAYING ABOUT	HOW THIS PRAYER WAS ANSWERED
_____	_____ _____ _____	_____ _____ _____
DATE	I'M PRAYING ABOUT	HOW THIS PRAYER WAS ANSWERED
_____	_____ _____ _____	_____ _____ _____

DATE   I'M PRAYING ABOUT   HOW THIS PRAYER WAS ANSWERED

_____   _____   _____

           _____   _____

           _____   _____

DATE   I'M PRAYING ABOUT   HOW THIS PRAYER WAS ANSWERED

_____   _____   _____

           _____   _____

           _____   _____

DATE   I'M PRAYING ABOUT   HOW THIS PRAYER WAS ANSWERED

_____   _____   _____

           _____   _____

           _____   _____

DATE   I'M PRAYING ABOUT   HOW THIS PRAYER WAS ANSWERED

_____   _____   _____

           _____   _____

           _____   _____

DATE   I'M PRAYING ABOUT   HOW THIS PRAYER WAS ANSWERED

_____   _____   _____

           _____   _____

           _____   _____

DATE	I'M PRAYING ABOUT	HOW THIS PRAYER WAS ANSWERED

DATE	I'M PRAYING ABOUT	HOW THIS PRAYER WAS ANSWERED

DATE	I'M PRAYING ABOUT	HOW THIS PRAYER WAS ANSWERED

DATE	I'M PRAYING ABOUT	HOW THIS PRAYER WAS ANSWERED

DATE	I'M PRAYING ABOUT	HOW THIS PRAYER WAS ANSWERED

Dear Friend,

You've come to the end of the Prayer Path, but I hope you'll keep praying and writing your prayers to God.

You can use a spiral notebook, or loose papers to write your prayers—just about anything will do. God doesn't need fancy paper to hear your prayers.

Trust God to listen, and pray often!

Karen Hill